Rookie
Read-About® Math

Springtime
Addition

By Jill Fuller

Consultant
Linda Bullock
Math Curriculum Specialist

Children's Press®
A Division of Scholastic Inc.
New York Toronto London Auckland Sydney
Mexico City New Delhi Hong Kong
Danbury, Connecticut

Designer: Herman Adler Design
Photo Researcher: Caroline Anderson
The photo on the cover shows butterflies.

Library of Congress Cataloging-in-Publication Data

Fuller, Jill, 1949-
  Springtime addition / by Jill Fuller.
    p. cm. — (Rookie read-about math)
  Includes bibliographical references and index.
  ISBN 0-516-24422-1 (lib. bdg.)   0-516-24668-2 (pbk.)
  1. Addition—Juvenile literature. I. Title. II. Series.
  QA115.F9265 2004
  513.2'11—dc22

                              2004005017

CHILDREN'S PRESS, and ROOKIE READ-ABOUT®,
and associated logos are trademarks and or registered trademarks
of Scholastic Library Publishing. SCHOLASTIC and associated logos
are trademarks and or registered trademarks of Scholastic Inc.

1 2 3 4 5 6 7 8 9 10 R 13 12 11 10 09 08 07 06 05 04

It is spring.

This is a field of orange poppies.

There is a lot to see, smell, and hear in the spring.

Look around. You might see a butterfly.

How many do you see?

Here are some more
butterflies.

How many do you see?

Now add all the butterflies together.

1 butterfly + 2 butterflies =

3 butterflies

Smell the springtime air. This girl loves to smell flowers.

Red and yellow daylilies

These flowers are different. How many do you see?

Here are some more
flowers.

How many do you see?

Red camellia flowers

Now add all the
flowers together.

4 flowers + 2 flowers =

6 flowers

Now, stop and listen. Do you hear the ducks quacking?

A bufflehead mother and her ducklings

These ducks are different.
How many do you see?

Here are some more ducks.
How many do you see?

Ducklings

Now add all the ducks together.

7 ducks + 3 ducks =

10 ducks

Look up to the sky.
You might see a kite.

These kites are different.
How many do you see?

Look, there are more kites.
How many do you see?

25

Now add all the kites together.

3 kites + 7 kites =

10 kites

Look around you in
the spring.

Can you think of more
things you can see, smell,
and hear?

Now, add them up!

Words You Know

butterfly

ducklings

flower

kite

spring

31

Index

About the Author

Jill Fuller is a teacher, writer, editor, and musician in Taos, New Mexico. She likes math, dogs, and springtime.

Photo Credits

Photographs © 2004: Corbis Images: 13, 14 right, 15 bottom, 31 top (Michael Boys), 25, 26 right, 27 bottom (Wolfgang Kaehler), 6, 8 right, 9 bottom, 17, 20 left, 21 top (George D. Lepp), 23, 26 left, 27 top, 31 bottom left (Roy Morsch), 10, 11, 14 left, 15 top, 19, 20 right, 21 bottom, 30 bottom (Royalty-Free), 16 (Norbert Schaefer), 3, 29, 31 bottom right (Brenda Tharp); PhotoEdit/Michael Newman: 5, 8 left, 9 top, 30 top; PunchStock/Photodisc: cover; Stone/Getty Images/Don Smetzer: 22.